Mindy Lott

Dear Friend: God Understands

A Motivational Memoir About the Makings of Mindy

Dear Friend: God Understands

Dear Friend: God Understands

Copyright © 2021 Mindy Lott

All rights reserved. No part of this book may be reproduced in any form without permission of the publisher/author.

References:

The Holy Bible AMP

The Holy Bible NIV

Dear Friend: God Understands

Dedicated to my precious angel baby. And to my daughter Madi, I love you more than life itself. You are the light of my life, the very person who teaches me to be relentless and tenacious in any and everything I do.

Dear Friend: God Understands

Contents

Introduction

Chapter 1 - Growing Up

Chapter 2 - Biology

Chapter 3 - Love

Chapter 4 - This Half Has Not Been Told

Chapter 5 - Identity

Chapter 6 - Made for This

Chapter 7 - Connecting the Dots

Prayer

Scripture Listing

Dear Friend: God Understands

Introduction

Dear Friend,

As you read through the pages of this book it is my prayer that you are inspired, find healing, and liberation. I want you to know that you are loved, you are valued, you are enough. You are not what hurt you, you are not the pain that has cut you deeply. You are everything that God says you are and throughout this book I will reaffirm His thoughts towards you. We were all created on purpose for a purpose! Sometimes you go through things and you feel that you are all alone. I am here to tell you that you are not! You are not alone and you will never be. Everything is working for the greater good. Regardless of what you may be experiencing, God understands!

Dear Friend: God Understands

"Every good thing given and every perfect gift is from above" James 1:17 AMP

Chapter One
Growing Up

Let's imagine it's March 25, 1991 it's the day that I was born. I was the fifth of five children and most of my memory is of my siblings being preteen and teenagers as I was growing up. We are all different in many ways yet we were so much alike, still today. I was a pretty happy child for the most part. I enjoyed playing outside, playing with barbies, and I loved to play "house", which is probably why I enjoy cooking and cleaning so much today!

I did not know that I would start to face adversities at a young age that would carry themselves into other areas of my life. Most of it was at school but some were in the home as well. I was told I didn't have "good hair" that my hair was "nappy" and my smile was not appealing. There were even kids who picked on me because of my skin. Countless times I heard "you think you're pretty because you're light skinned or you act like a white girl" whatever that was supposed to mean. I started thinking maybe my hair is nappy? Perhaps my teeth aren't nice?

Looking back at pictures pre-high school I would smile but I never showed teeth, I became very insecure about that. In 2006 we lost everything to a house fire. I was in the 9th grade, about 14 at the time and there was this one girl who always referred to me as "chicken little" deviously implying that my neck was long since I was always pretty slim. I know it might seem small, but imagine being just a kid with these things playing in the background of your head when you are still growing into who you are supposed to be.

If I could say anything to my younger self it would be that you are beautiful, you are strong, you are more than enough because the God in you is more than enough. Your hair is beautiful, your smile is one that lights up a room! It is indeed one of your greatest physical attributes! The things that are said to you and about you won't matter when you know who you are. You are God's creation. The only things that can remain prevalent in our lives are the things that we give the authority to. To every little girl or boy, I encourage you to love yourself more, to tune out negativity, and embrace everything you consider a flaw because it is what makes you unique.

A note to my younger self:

Dear Friend: God Understands

Dear Friend: God Understands

"See what an incredible quality of love the Father has shown to us, that we would be named and called and counted the children of God!" - 1 John 3:1 AMP

Chapter Two
Biology

What comes to mind when you think of family? For a brief moment I would like for you to reflect on what family means to you before you continue to read. Is it two people who have a child together? Or is it having someone to love you unconditionally in spite of your shortcomings? To me, family is support, family is love, family is a choice, family is belonging even if DNA is not the same.

When I was 16 years old, I was informed that the man whom I loved and adored my entire life was not my biological father. I felt as if my life until this point was a lie. I did not want to believe it and for so long I could not even understand it. How could he not be my father when he displays love? He fathered my other siblings but not me? While he was not "hands on " or physically present every single day he always displayed unconditional love, he never spoke negatively to me, and that is what I came to care about. My daddy chose me, he literally chose me and I truly believe he loved me every single day until the day God called him home. There was never any significance to me as to why he was no longer married to my mother, or why he may or may not have been able to have stability in the workplace. He loved me, he saw me and for most of my childhood and some of my adult life all I ever wanted was to be seen.

Feeling seen can look different to each person, most importantly we have to have the fulfillment within ourselves! His untimely passing affected me in ways I never talked much about. I continually went back and forth with myself with questions that I will at no time have the answers to ever and that's ok. I have learned to be alright with the unchangeable and hold onto the memories of him that I have and that is love. I often reflect on the scripture, "I know you before I formed you in your mother's womb." Jeremiah 1:5. So even when I did not think I knew myself because of biology He knew who I was and He knows who you are too! He knows you; He loves you.

Dear Friend: God Understands

Readers Notes:

Dear Friend: God Understands

Dear Friend: God Understands

"Above all things guard your heart, for everything you do flows from it" – Proverbs 4:23 NIV

Chapter Three

Love

In the book of first Corinthians 13:4 the Apostle Paul says. "Love is patient, love is kind. It does not envy, it does not boast, it is not proud. It is not rude, it is not self-seeking, it is not easily angered." I have always been what one would call a hopeless romantic. In the past, I absolutely loved the idea of being in love and thought of it as if it was a fairytale, but the truth of the matter is that nothing is right? I spent my entire teenage years and early to mid-twenties in a relationship that was no longer serving me. I don't state that in the physical aspect, but one that was uplifting, adding value, granting warranty, and security. It was not all bad, until this day I'll say that I have spent some of the best times of my life in this relationship.

He was my best friend, my first love, and the first person I came to care about romantically. I truly loved him with my entire being, but it still was not enough to overshadow the infidelity, the deceit, and pain I was experiencing internally. Love just simply was not enough. No one knew just how awful things really were after the first 4 years in. It was covered up with cute photos, dates, and gifts. But let me tell you, no matter what is purchased or given it can never amount to your peace of mind!

Love is not making the same "mistakes" countless times. It is not allowing your partner to question their worth. Love is not disrespect, seen or unseen. I found myself so mentally exhausted that I became unrecognizable to myself. I literally felt like I did not know who I was anymore. I remember so vividly being at a youth explosion a few years back. I was so broken, so lost, I was so confused. The woman ministering that evening began to pray and my heart was so connected to the prayer she stopped and called me to the front of the sanctuary. She said to me "I do not know who he is but he lied to you, he deceived you, and God wants you to know that what you need is not in that person but in Him." It was like she was reading the pages of my heart. She also told me that God was going to give me a vision and an ear to the stories of other young girls. At the time I was still unsure of who I was or where I was going, so I didn't fully comprehend all that she said to me during that time. If you'll just keep reading, I will tell you how the prophecy came to fruition. Growing up I sometimes saw my mom struggle. I came from an unconventional upbringing and broken family dynamic. I wanted so badly, more than anything to give my daughter what I never had. When the relationship failed, I felt like I had failed my daughter until I realized she needed me. How can I show up for my daughter every day when I don't have the courage to show up for myself?

Friend, walking away from a relationship, friendship, job, or anything that no longer serves you is not a sign of weakness but of bravery. How daringly beautiful was it for me to feel liberated in myself after so long, because after all the times I was choosing "us" I made the decision to choose me!

I affirm that I will no longer accept things or people that are no longer positively contributing to my life:

Dear Friend: God Understands

Dear Friend: God Understands

"For I know the plans and thoughts that I have for you,' says the Lord, 'plans for peace and well-being and not for disaster, to give you a future and a hope." -Jeremiah 29:11 AMP

Chapter Four

This Half Has Not Been Told

When I was just 20 years old, I found out I was pregnant with my daughter. I can recall exactly where I was and the numbness, I felt all of my body. So many thoughts traveled through my mind. I just could not believe it and I honestly felt like my life was over. After informing my close family and friends I thought I would feel more relieved as I was in need of support, but that was not the initial outcome.

A family member said to me "you are stupid, you will never be anything, I will give you money for an abortion but if you keep "it" you'll never receive another penny from me." They were so close to me the saliva from their mouth was all over my face. I shed so many tears this day, because more than anything in this moment I needed my loved ones to be there for me, to let me know it would be ok, but that did not happen. I made the decision that I would have my baby and go to school. I did not have to choose one or the other. I knew it would be difficult but I was looking forward to all that motherhood would bring.

Have you ever been driving for a period of time and once you've reached your destination you think to yourself, "how did I make it?". Would you believe me if I told you I felt like that for nearly 2 years of my life? As I was matriculating through my undergraduate institution, I also worked a full-time job. I would work 32 to 38 hours a week, go to school 3 to 4 nights a week until 10pm all while being a mother to my daughter. There were instances where I would take her to class with me if I did not have a babysitter, because really – how bad do you want it? My very last semester I was required to complete a 400-hour internship. I worked full time hours on my job and completed 40-45 hours on my internship which collectively were 80-hour weeks.

I honestly did not know if I was going or coming and truthfully at times I wanted to die because never waking up again seemed to be better than the pain I was feeling. I was depressed, I was sleep deprived, I had no appetite, I didn't look like myself, my relationship was failing, and I was trying to be the best mother I could be. I was beginning to be consumed by everything around me and I cried so much it felt like I was drinking my tears. I had lost so much weight and to make things worse people made comments like "you're so skinny you need to eat" or "that baby weighs more than you". Oh, how I deeply wanted to have an appetite but it just wasn't there.

I look back now and use this as a teachable moment. I have learned to be a lot kinder to myself and to others because the outward appearance only scratches the surface of what someone is dealing with internally. I began developing body dysmorphia looking at myself in the mirror naked, I was literally skin and bone. My ribs were so visibly noticeable and all I could do was cry. I'd wake up some mornings, laying in my bed and thinking, "I woke up again?".

But my daughter, oh my sweet daughter, she saved me.

My daughter literally saved my life. Every time I wanted to give up, I would see her precious face and I knew that I had so much more to live for. I began reading my bible more and being more intentional with my prayer life. God loves us, He loves us so much that He sent His only son Jesus to die for us. One of my many favorite scriptures says, "You will keep him in perfect peace whose mind is stayed on Him because he trusts You" -Isaiah 26:3. The mind is the starting place for behavior.

While we cannot control what comes to our mind, we can control which thoughts we hold hostage. During this period of my life, it was important for me to feed my mind with upright things. Accepting and honoring only what I could control and allowing God to work out the remainder of my issues. Friend, feed your mind with positive things because having a peaceful mind requires you to keep your mind on the right things.

It is important for us not to take in everything that is going on in our lives because it will overwhelm you. You may not be able to see it right now, but trust me there is nothing that you are facing that is too hard for God. He brought me through some of my most difficult times and I know He will do it for you too. The initial step is just to trust Him, He already knows your very thoughts, your feelings. We don't have it all together and we never will but when we have Jesus, He can hold us together.

Today, I will take the first step in keeping my mind on the right things:

_____

_____

_____

_____

_____

_____

_____

_____

_____

_____

_____

Dear Friend: God Understands

Dear Friend: God Understands

"I will be a Father to you, and you will be my sons and daughters, says the Lord Almighty."

-2 Corinthians 6:18 NIV

Chapter Five

Identity

For some time, I had searched for my identity. Identity is more than the physical qualities that one possesses. It is truly knowing who you are from the inside out. I was unaware of who I was due to some of my past sufferings and societal standards. I went to church Sunday after Sunday hearing God's word but still not truly knowing who I was in Him.

I came to know Jesus when I was 9 years old. While I have strayed away from Him several times, He has always been waiting for me to come back home. I think about the story of the prodigal son and how his father was ready to welcome him with open arms filled with compassion. I felt like I made decisions so terribly that I could never come back to Him. The idea of my sins rested so heavily causing me to feel great embarrassment and shame.

My identity could never be found in my family, a relationship, a job, or money – nothing tangible. Did you know that He doesn't care how many times you mess up? He doesn't care how many times you fall short. He will always be the most consistent part of your life. Once I came to know that my identity lies in Him, I discovered my purpose. When you walk in purpose your desires change. Knowing who you are will keep you from seeking validation from others, it will allow you to accept less, and most importantly when you know who you are in Him you will only be about His business.

What do you believe about your identity? What is one practice you can implement to grow your relationship with God?

_____

_____

_____

_____

_____

_____

_____

_____

_____

Dear Friend: God Understands

Dear Friend: God Understands

"For the Spirit God gave us does not make us timid, but gives us power, love and self-discipline." 2 Timothy 1:7 NIV

Chapter Six

Made for This

If you're reading this chapter then you know that I talked briefly about a prophecy that was given to me a few years ago. A principal reached out to myself and some coworkers to speak to the youth at his alternative school. The students enrolled at this school were placed there if they were unable to attend regular school for a variety of reasons. The initial meeting was a success and it became an outgoing partnership.

When I began speaking to the girls I would be so connected to their stories and I saw so much of myself inside of them. I had no idea that this was the unfolding of the prophecy given to me a few years prior. I recall laying in my bed several nights and I could not sleep. Every time I would lay down for the evening God would continue to fill me up with ideas and promises that I have since been able to see come to pass. It was when I began to understand this was the word spoken into my life previously. He instructed me on recruitment strategies for my mentees, what to tell them, and even what to name the mentorship program. If you would have asked me some years ago if I would be leading a group of young girls, I would have thought you were losing it, literally.

I just never saw myself being that person. I would say ugly things about myself, things that were unpleasant and very self-deprecating, but He showed me that I was made for this. It takes a person with heart, passion, and obedience for these assignments. Starting my mentoring program has been one of the most rewarding things I have ever done. I get to see the positive transformations made in their lives, I see walls of insecurities being torn down and self-esteem being built up, I see young girls giving back and serving their community so selflessly. I see God's idea; I see His promises. Before, I did not know that every little thing I encountered was preparing me for this exact moment.

I have learned to pray God's will for my life and not my own. Even when I do not feel like I have what it takes I remember that it's God's idea and that He chose me. If He can choose me that means I have whatever it takes or He will provide me with the things that I need.

Friend, I know that the thought of certain things can be scary, especially when you may feel incompetent, but I am here to tell you that you were made for this! You will always be protected when you walk in purpose. What a difference it makes to wake up with your purpose on our mind and instead of your insecurities.

I have been exclusively designed for my purpose. Today I choose to release my fears and doubts starting with:

_____

_____

_____

_____

_____

_____

_____

_____

_____

_____

Dear Friend: God Understands

Dear Friend: God Understands

"And we know that in all things God works for the good of those who love him, who[a] have been called according to his purpose" -Romans 8:28 NIV

Chapter Seven

Connecting the Dots

Dear Friend: God Understands

I believe that experience is one of the best teachers. You need your valley; you can't walk someone through anything you haven't been through. We can take our trials and traumas and allow them to take control of our lives or we can use them to fuel purpose and help someone else. There is nothing that happens in our life that catches Him by surprise. I know that some of my story may seem painful, and truthfully, I still get very emotional thinking about it. Not because it makes me sad but because God brought me through the darkest times in my life and it makes my heart completely full that I am able to share some of my most intimate parts unapologetically. I have had low self-esteem, I have been heartbroken, I have been depressed, but I learned to lean on His understanding and not my own. Quite often I did not trust people when I was hurting because I felt like everyone was out to hurt me which wasn't true. One of the first steps in the healing process is to acknowledge your pain and/or embarrassment.

It is important to come to terms with what has happened as long as you do not stay there. When I began therapy, one of the things I learned quickly is that it is ok to be in touch with our feelings as long as we do not allow them to consume our lives.

Secondly, is the big F word, forgiveness. I know what might have happened seems so bad that you think you can't forgive. You can't stop thinking about it, you buy yourself something nice to make you feel better momentarily, you lose sleep over it, you can't eat, or you are overeating to suppress your feelings, I know. Ephesians 4:32 says, "be kind and compassionate to one another, forgiving just as Christ forgave you". Forgiveness is only possible when you willingly cooperate. I chose to forgive those who hurt me both knowingly and unknowingly for my own peace of mind. Walking around with unforgiveness in your heart is a lot heavier than forgiving someone especially when you're walking in purpose because God can't flow freely through a hardened heart. Forgiveness is accepting that some people will never apologize.

How a person treats you is a direct reflection of who they are, not who you are. But it cannot be done without compassion. Do not focus on having compassion for your offender, but have compassion for their pain that allows them to make choices that result in hurt. You are responsible for letting go so that you can move forward. We can hold onto things for years and it can contaminate other areas of our lives. Some journeys to healing are a lot longer than others but the outcome and destination is what is most rewarding because the more our pain consumes us the more it controls us.

My therapist challenged me to write a letter to a person who hurt me as if I was giving it to them. I keep it in a sacred place but the best part about it is I was able to release feelings that had been bottled up inside. Friend, I challenge you to do the same.

Open your heart and your mind and allow every feeling to fall on that paper.

Believe me when I say that nothing you have encountered will ever be wasted. God will use the things that the enemy has told you disqualifies you. I have been asked, "if you could change one thing about your life, would you?" my answer is no. I would not change anything. If I had never had these encounters, I would never be in a position to encourage you. My understandings have opened many doors for me, they have helped shape and mold me in numerous ways. I am grateful for it all. Friend, always remember that it's not where you are. It is where you are headed. Never mind the naysayers, God will weed them out. For every test, there is a testimony that explains His favor, grace, and mercy. Let's choose peace over pain, triumph over trauma, and healing over hurt because no matter what you are facing God understands!

Everything I have encountered up until this moment was necessary to get me where I am. Every detail of my life has been for myself and to shed light for others. All things are working for the greater good. Everyone has a story to tell. What will be yours?

Dear Friend: God Understands

Dear Friend: God Understands

Dear Friend: God Understands

Dear Friend: God Understands

Dear Friend: God Understands

Dear Friend: God Understands

Dear Friend: God Understands

Prayer

Lord, I thank you for this time of supplication and prayer. I thank you for this reader. I thank you for such divine intention. Thank you for creating us on purpose for a purpose. I pray that you will continue to help us see ourselves in the light that you see us. We are grateful for the gentle reminders you always send. Thank you for letting us know that you've got us on your mind and you will provide comfort in our suffering. Life gets busy but you are never too busy for us. Thank you for giving us what we don't deserve, we appreciate your grace and your mercy for there is none like You. Please give us the desire to have you more than anything or anyone. Lord, help us to stay focused and along the path that you have created for us, and even when we fall thank you for always welcoming us back with open arms. I pray that sharing my truth and encounters will allow them to see You. We release everything from our hearts that may keep us from seeing the fullness of life and the fullness of You. We grab on to your unconditional love and kindness. We believe what your word says about us. We thank you; we love you, and we count it all done in your son Jesus name, Amen!

Dear Friend: God Understands

A list of Mindy's favorite scriptures

- Proverbs 4:23
- Psalms 91
- Philippians 4:13
- Philippians 4:7
- Galatians 6:10
- Psalms 36:9
- Romans 8:28
- Romans 8:26
- Romans 8:37
- Jeremiah 29:11
- Isaiah 26:3
- Deuteronomy 31:6
- Exodus 14:4

Dear Friend: God Understands

- Isaiah 55:8
- John 14:14
- Ephesians 6:10
- 2 Timothy 1:7

www.ingramcontent.com/pod-product-compliance
Lightning Source LLC
Chambersburg PA
CBHW071838290426
44109CB00017B/1847